I0828202

THIS BOOK BELONGS TO:

WELCOME TO
SOUTH CAROLINA

Dedicated to all the explorers.

ISBN 978-1-958985-84-7

www.joeysavestheday.com

A Mimi Book

South Carolina is named after King Charles of England, whose Latin name was Carolus. The area was originally called Carolina, and when the colony was later divided into two, the lower portion became South Carolina, simply meaning the southern part of Carolina.

South Carolina has a long and important history that began with Native American nations such as the Cherokee and Catawba. European explorers arrived in the 1500s, and the English established the first permanent settlement at Charleston in 1670. The colony grew through farming and trade, and later played a major role in the American Revolution. South Carolina was also the first state to secede from the Union in 1860, which helped start the Civil War at Fort Sumter in 1861.

South Carolina was the eighth state to join the Union. It officially joined on May 23, 1788.

8th

South Carolina is located in the Southeastern region of the United States. It is bordered by North Carolina and Georgia, and it also touches the Atlantic Ocean.

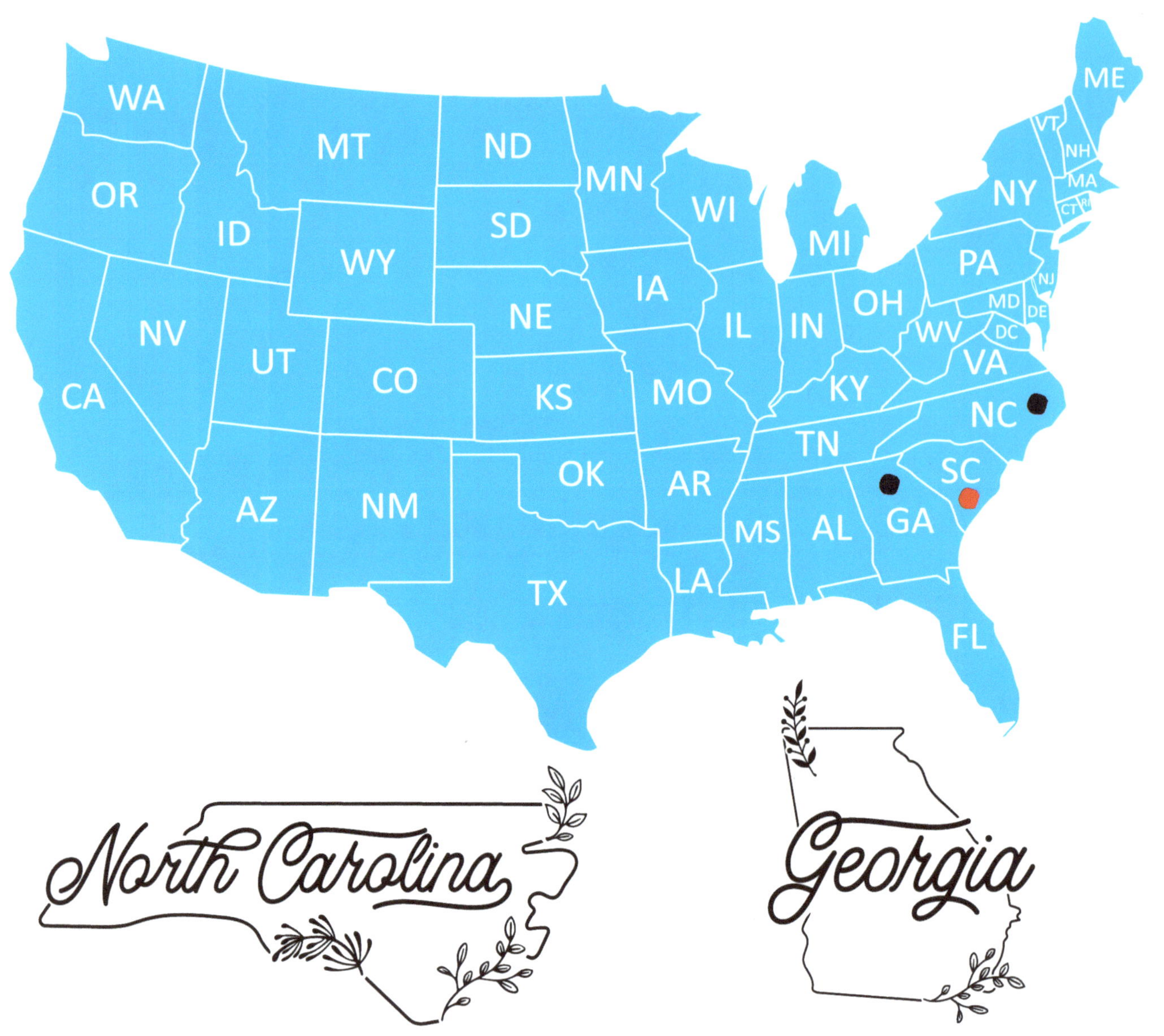

South Carolina's state flag was officially adopted in 1861.

A couple of South Carolina's nicknames include the Palmetto State and the Swamp State.

ST8

ST8

South Carolina's state motto is actually two mottos: "Animis Opibusque Parati," meaning "Prepared in Mind and Resources," and "Dum Spiro Spero," meaning "While I Breathe, I Hope." Both mottos were adopted in 1776.

The abbreviation for South Carolina is SC.

Columbia is the capital of South Carolina.
It officially became the capital in 1786.

Columbia, South Carolina, has an estimated population of about 144,000 people.

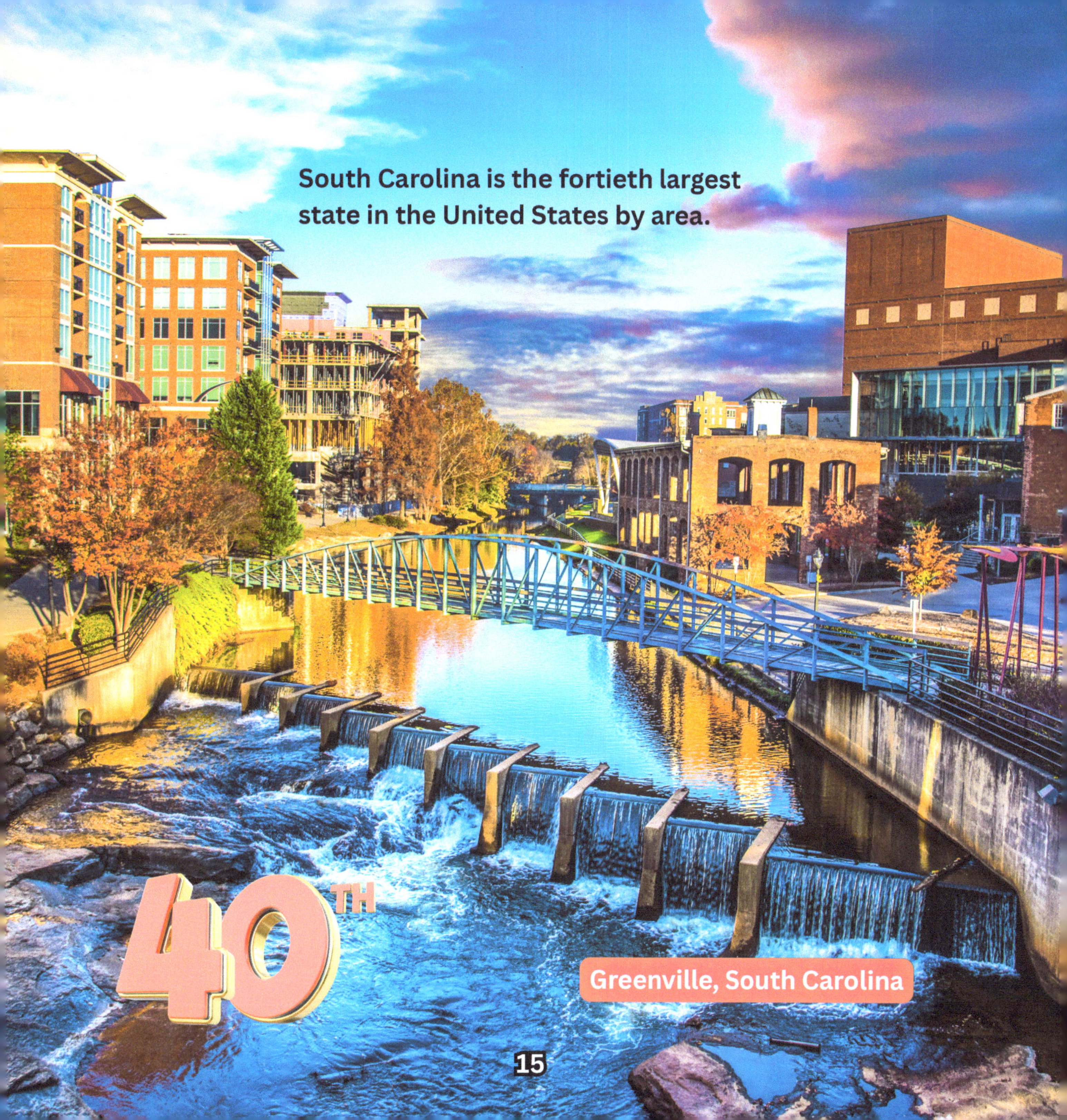

South Carolina is the fortieth largest state in the United States by area.

Greenville, South Carolina

There are approximately 5,470,000 people residing in the state of South Carolina.

Beaufort, South Carolina

SOUTH Carolina

There are 46 counties in South Carolina.

Here is a list of twenty of those counties:

Abbeville
Aiken
Anderson
Bamberg
Barnwell
Beaufort
Berkeley
Calhoun
Charleston
Cherokee
Chester
Clarendon
Colleton
Darlington
Dillon
Dorchester
Edgefield
Fairfield
Florence
Georgetown

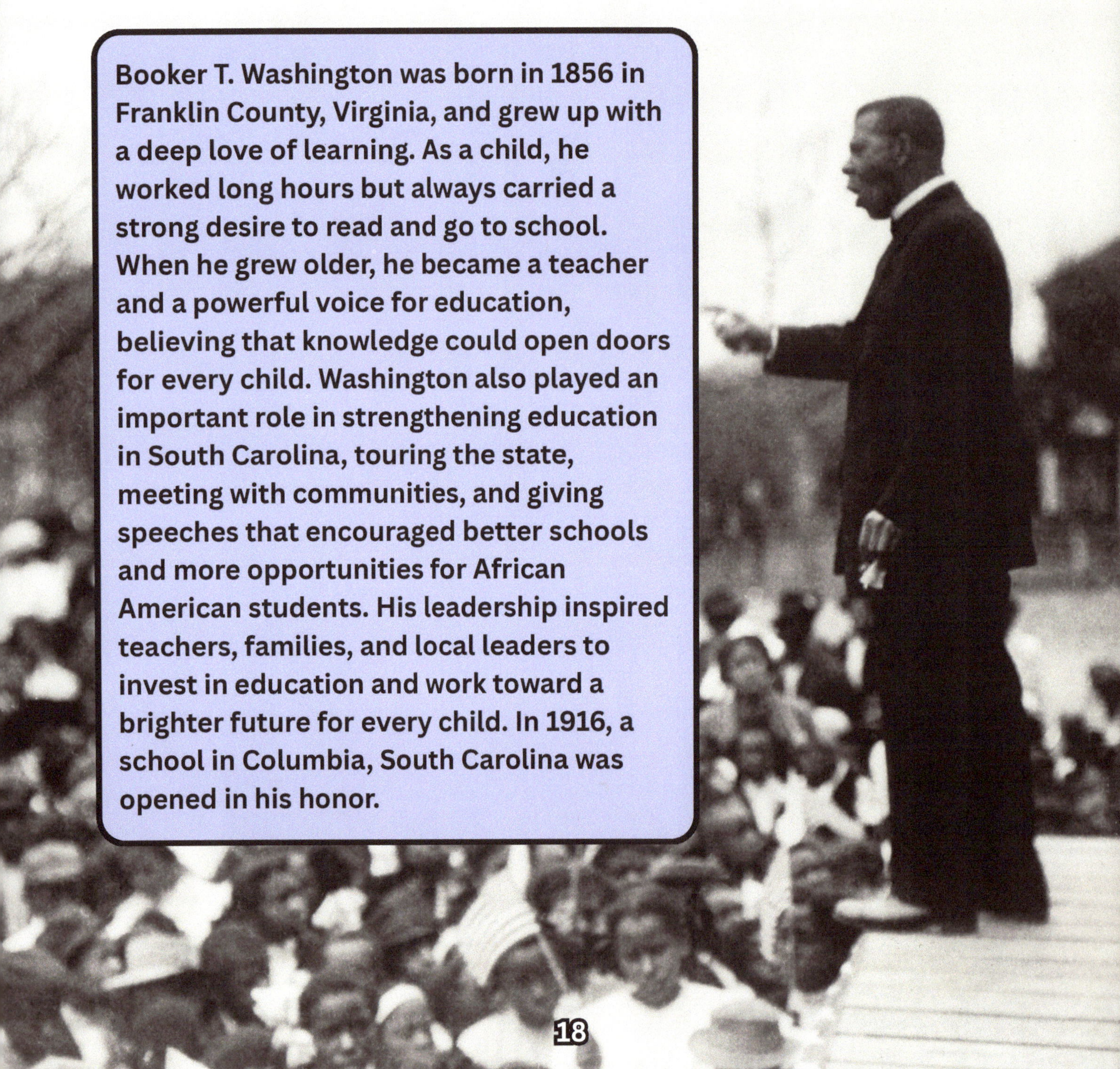

Booker T. Washington was born in 1856 in Franklin County, Virginia, and grew up with a deep love of learning. As a child, he worked long hours but always carried a strong desire to read and go to school. When he grew older, he became a teacher and a powerful voice for education, believing that knowledge could open doors for every child. Washington also played an important role in strengthening education in South Carolina, touring the state, meeting with communities, and giving speeches that encouraged better schools and more opportunities for African American students. His leadership inspired teachers, families, and local leaders to invest in education and work toward a brighter future for every child. In 1916, a school in Columbia, South Carolina was opened in his honor.

Andrew Jackson was born on March 15, 1767, in the Waxhaws region along the border of North Carolina and South Carolina. He grew up on the rugged frontier, where life was tough and families worked hard to survive. Jackson later became a soldier, a lawyer, and eventually the 7th President of the United States.

Station Cove Falls is a gentle, fan-shaped waterfall at Oconee Station State Historic Site in northwestern South Carolina. A short, easy trail leads families through a quiet forest to the wide cascade, where water slips over smooth rock layers into a shallow pool. With its peaceful setting and nearby historic buildings, it's a favorite spot for a simple, relaxing nature walk.

The Liberty Bridge is a modern pedestrian bridge located in downtown Greenville's Falls Park on the Reedy. Opened in 2004, it is known for its unique curved design and its single suspension tower, which makes the bridge appear to float above the waterfall below. The bridge is 345 feet long and offers clear views of the Reedy River Falls, making it one of Greenville's most popular landmarks.

The Angel Oak Tree on Johns Island is one of the oldest and largest living oak trees in the United States. It is estimated to be 400–500 years old, and its branches stretch more than 160 feet across the ground. The tree stands about 65 feet tall and provides an enormous shaded area beneath its canopy. The Angel Oak is a protected natural landmark and is one of South Carolina's most famous symbols of strength, history, and natural beauty.

The official state flower of South Carolina is the Yellow Jessamine. It was chosen as the state flower in 1924.

The palmetto tree is South Carolina's state tree. Its soft trunk and fan-shaped leaves make it a familiar sight along the coast. The palmetto was officially adopted on March 17, 1939, and today it appears on the state flag as a symbol of strength and coastal beauty.

Mount Pleasant, South Carolina.

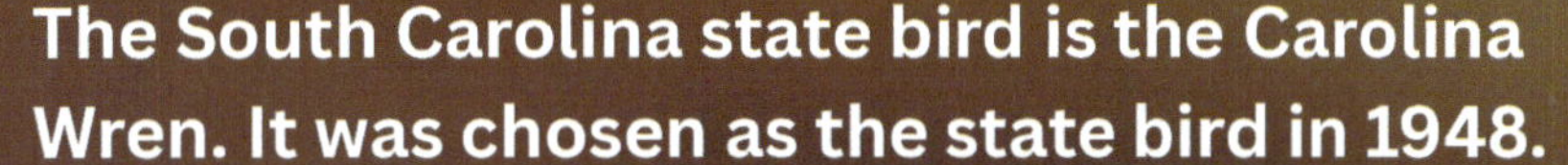

The South Carolina state bird is the Carolina Wren. It was chosen as the state bird in 1948.

The striped bass is South Carolina's state fish. It's a strong, silvery fish with bold dark stripes that make it easy to recognize in lakes and rivers. The striped bass was officially adopted as the state fish in 1972.

Some animals that live in South Carolina are white-tailed deer, black bears, red foxes, bobcats, and great blue herons.

The Riverbanks Zoo & Garden is located in Columbia, South Carolina, and is home to hundreds of animals from around the world. Kids can see lions, koalas, giraffes, penguins, and playful primates, along with colorful birds and reptiles.

Some crops grown in South Carolina are peaches, corn, soybeans, and cotton.

ENJOY

Shrimp and grits is one of South Carolina's most iconic dishes. It began as a simple fisherman's breakfast along the coast, where fresh shrimp were cooked with creamy, buttery grits. Over time, it became a favorite meal across the state. Today, families enjoy it in many different styles, from classic and simple to fancy restaurant versions, but it always celebrates South Carolina's coastal flavors.

South Carolina experiences a wide range of temperatures throughout the year. The hottest temperature ever recorded in the state was 113 degrees Fahrenheit, measured in Johnston on June 29, 2012. On the opposite end, the coldest temperature documented was −19 degrees Fahrenheit, recorded in Caesars Head on January 21, 1985.

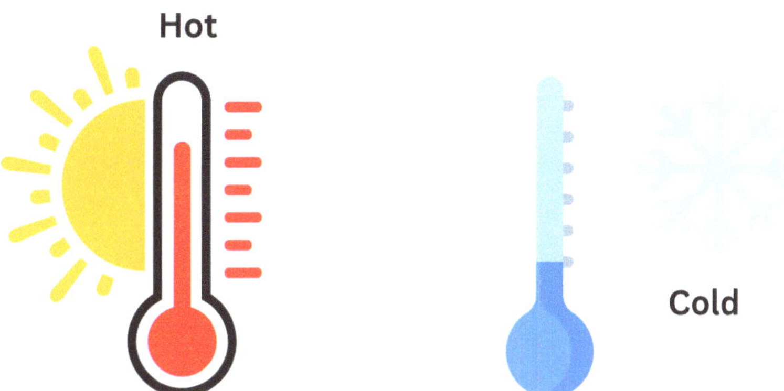

The largest airport in South Carolina is Charleston International Airport, located in North Charleston, near the beautiful coastal city of Charleston. It sits at 5500 International Boulevard and serves as the main travel hub for people flying in and out of the state. This airport connects travelers to cities all across the country.

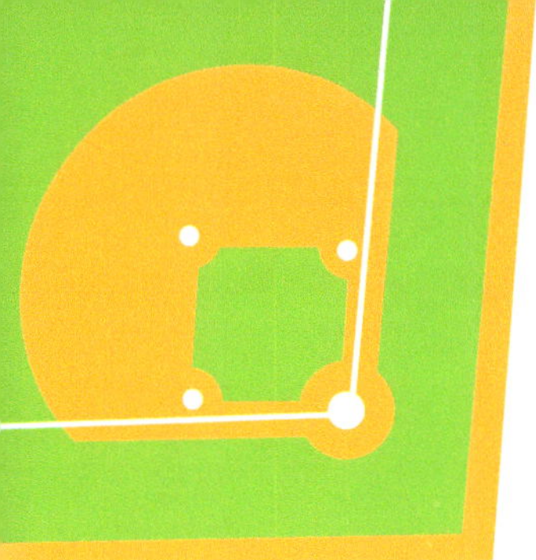

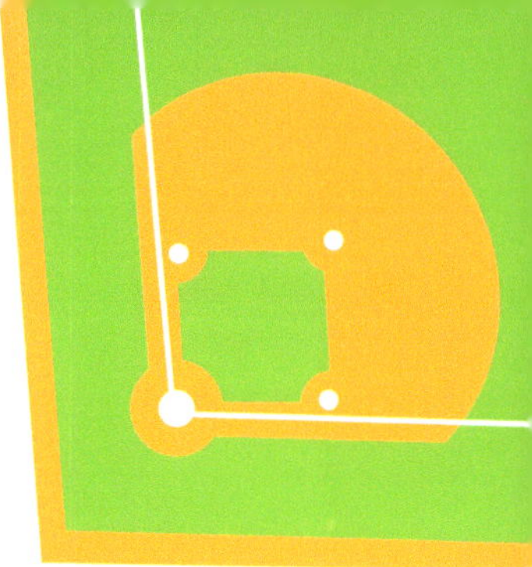

The Charleston RiverDogs are a Minor League Baseball team based in Charleston, right along the beautiful South Carolina coast. They play their home games at Joseph P. Riley, Jr. Park, a bright and cheerful ballpark known for its fun atmosphere and great views of the marsh. The RiverDogs are the Single-A affiliate of the Tampa Bay Rays, which means many future major-league players spend time on this team as they grow their skills.

FOOTBALL

The Carolina Panthers are one of the most well-known football teams connected to South Carolina, and many of their fans live throughout the state. The team plays its home games at Bank of America Stadium in nearby Charlotte, a loud and energetic place filled with cheering fans wearing bright blue and black. The Panthers are known for their exciting game-day atmosphere, their proud "Keep Pounding" motto, and the way their fans come together to support the team.

Can you name these?

I hope you enjoyed learning about South Carolina.

To explore fun facts about the other 49 states, visit my website at www.joeysavestheday.com. You'll also find a wide variety of homeschool resources to support joyful learning at home. If you enjoyed this book, I would be grateful if you left a review. Your feedback truly helps. Thank you for your support!

Check out these other interesting books in the 50 States Fact Books Series!

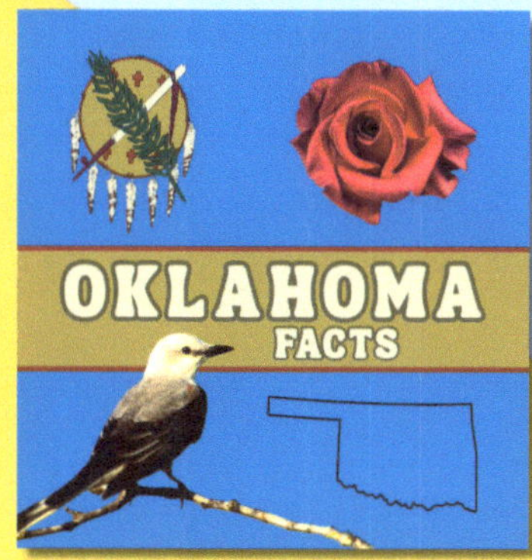

www.mimibooks.com